CRICKET

Journal

NAME _____

SEASON YEAR _____

TEAM NAME _____

My Cricket Journal

-Cricket-

My Cricket Journal

-Cricket-

CRICKET *Journal* SECTIONS

01 Season Goals
Write down your Top 3 Season Goals

02 Training & Game Logbook
Record your training sessions and game details

03 Season Notes
Write further details of your season to keep a record for future reference

04 Autographs & Photos
Gather the autographs and photos of team members, coaches and famous players

01

SEASON GOALS

01 CRICKET SEASON GOALS

GOAL 1

· ·

· ·

· ·

GOAL 2

· ·

· ·

· ·

GOAL 3

· ·

· ·

· ·

My Cricket Journal

-Cricket-

02

TRAINING & GAME LOGBOOK

TRAINING

Date: / /   **Start time**   :

End time   :

Skills Completed
Write down the skills you worked on and developed during your training sessions.

....

....

....

....

Skills to improve
Write down areas that you can improve on for your next training session

....

....

....

....

Coach & Team Focus
Write down if your coach or team has a skill or game focus you are working on

....

....

Extra Notes
Do you have additional notes or thoughts you would like to write down?

....

....

....

GAME DAY

Date: /   /   **Start time**   :

Location: ....

Home Game   ◯   **Away Game**   ◯

Game Details

.... **Vs** ....

Game Result   Runs   Runs

Our Score   **Opposition**

Overs Bowled:

Coach Feedback

....

....

....

My Performance

Write down how you felt you contributed to the game. Did the coach provide you any personal feedback? Did you have any highlights? Did you have areas of improvement?

....

....

....

....

....

....

TRAINING

Date: / /   **Start time**   :

End time   :

Skills Completed
Write down the skills you worked on and developed during your training sessions.

....

....

....

....

Skills to improve
Write down areas that you can improve on for your next training session

....

....

....

....

Coach & Team Focus
Write down if your coach or team has a skill or game focus you are working on

....

....

Extra Notes
Do you have additional notes or thoughts you would like to write down?

....

....

....

GAME DAY

Date: / / **Start time** :

Location: ....

Home Game ⚪ **Away Game** ⚪

Game Details

.... **Vs** ....

Game Result

| | Runs | | | Runs |

Our Score ☐ **Opposition** ☐

Overs Bowled:

Coach Feedback

....

....

....

My Performance

Write down how you felt you contributed to the game. Did the coach provide you any personal feedback? Did you have any highlights? Did you have areas of improvement?

....

....

....

....

....

....

TRAINING

Date: ___ / ___ / ___   **Start time** ___ : ___

End time ___ : ___

Skills Completed
Write down the skills you worked on and developed during your training sessions.

....

....

....

....

Skills to improve
Write down areas that you can improve on for your next training session

....

....

....

....

Coach & Team Focus
Write down if your coach or team has a skill or game focus you are working on

....

....

Extra Notes
Do you have additional notes or thoughts you would like to write down?

....

....

....

GAME DAY

Date: /   /   **Start time**   :

Location: ....

Home Game ⚪   **Away Game** ⚪

Game Details

.... **Vs** ....

Game Result   Runs   Runs

Our Score [   ]   **Opposition** [   ]

Overs Bowled:

Coach Feedback

....

....

....

My Performance

Write down how you felt you contributed to the game. Did the coach provide you any personal feedback? Did you have any highlights? Did you have areas of improvement?

....

....

....

....

....

....

TRAINING

Date: / /   **Start time**   :

                   End time   :

Skills Completed

Write down the skills you worked on and developed during your training sessions.

....

....

....

....

Skills to improve

Write down areas that you can improve on for your next training session

....

....

....

....

Coach & Team Focus

Write down if your coach or team has a skill or game focus you are working on

....

....

Extra Notes

Do you have additional notes or thoughts you would like to write down?

....

....

....

GAME DAY

Date: /   /   **Start time**   :

Location: ....

Home Game ⬤   **Away Game** ⬤

Game Details

.... **Vs** ....

Game Result   Runs   Runs

Our Score   **Opposition**

Overs Bowled:

Coach Feedback

....

....

....

My Performance

Write down how you felt you contributed to the game. Did the coach provide you any personal feedback? Did you have any highlights? Did you have areas of improvement?

....

....

....

....

....

....

TRAINING

Date: / / **Start time** :

End time :

Skills Completed
Write down the skills you worked on and developed during your training sessions.

....

....

....

....

Skills to improve
Write down areas that you can improve on for your next training session

....

....

....

....

Coach & Team Focus
Write down if your coach or team has a skill or game focus you are working on

....

....

Extra Notes
Do you have additional notes or thoughts you would like to write down?

....

....

....

GAME DAY

Date: /   /   **Start time**   :

Location: ....

Home Game 　　　**Away Game**

Game Details

.... **Vs** ....

Game Result   Runs   Runs

Our Score   **Opposition**

Overs Bowled:

Coach Feedback

....

....

....

My Performance   Write down how you felt you contributed to the game. Did
                       the coach provide you any personal feedback? Did you
                       have any highlights? Did you have areas of improvement?

....

....

....

....

....

....

TRAINING

Date: / /

Start time :

End time :

Skills Completed

Write down the skills you worked on and developed during your training sessions.

....

....

....

....

Skills to improve

Write down areas that you can improve on for your next training session

....

....

....

....

Coach & Team Focus

Write down if your coach or team has a skill or game focus you are working on

....

....

Extra Notes

Do you have additional notes or thoughts you would like to write down?

....

....

....

GAME DAY

Date: / /   **Start time** :

Location: ....

Home Game ◯   **Away Game** ◯

Game Details

.... **Vs** ....

Game Result   Runs   Runs

Our Score   **Opposition**

Overs Bowled:

Coach Feedback

....

....

....

My Performance   Write down how you felt you contributed to the game. Did the coach provide you any personal feedback? Did you have any highlights? Did you have areas of improvement?

....

....

....

....

....

....

TRAINING

Date: / /

Start time :

End time :

Skills Completed

Write down the skills you worked on and developed during your training sessions.

....

....

....

....

Skills to improve

Write down areas that you can improve on for your next training session

....

....

....

....

Coach & Team Focus

Write down if your coach or team has a skill or game focus you are working on

....

....

Extra Notes

Do you have additional notes or thoughts you would like to write down?

....

....

....

GAME DAY

Date: / / **Start time** :

Location: ....

Home Game ⬤ **Away Game** ⬤

Game Details

.... **Vs** ....

Game Result

Runs Runs

Our Score **Opposition**

Overs Bowled:

Coach Feedback

....

....

....

My Performance Write down how you felt you contributed to the game. Did the coach provide you any personal feedback? Did you have any highlights? Did you have areas of improvement?

....

....

....

....

....

....

TRAINING

Date: / /

Start time :

End time :

Skills Completed

Write down the skills you worked on and developed during your training sessions.

....

....

....

....

Skills to improve

Write down areas that you can improve on for your next training session

....

....

....

....

Coach & Team Focus

Write down if your coach or team has a skill or game focus you are working on

....

....

Extra Notes

Do you have additional notes or thoughts you would like to write down?

....

....

....

GAME DAY

Date: /   /   **Start time**   :

Location: ....

Home Game   **Away Game**

Game Details

.... **Vs** ....

Game Result   Runs   Runs

Our Score   **Opposition**

Overs Bowled:

Coach Feedback

....
....
....

My Performance   Write down how you felt you contributed to the game. Did the coach provide you any personal feedback? Did you have any highlights? Did you have areas of improvement?

....
....
....
....
....
....

TRAINING

Date: / /

Start time :

End time :

Skills Completed

Write down the skills you worked on and developed during your training sessions.

....

....

....

....

Skills to improve

Write down areas that you can improve on for your next training session

....

....

....

....

Coach & Team Focus

Write down if your coach or team has a skill or game focus you are working on

....

....

Extra Notes

Do you have additional notes or thoughts you would like to write down?

....

....

....

GAME DAY

Date: / /   **Start time**   :

Location: ....

Home Game ⬤   **Away Game** ⬤

Game Details

.... **Vs** ....

Game Result   Runs   Runs

Our Score   **Opposition**

Overs Bowled:

Coach Feedback

....

....

....

My Performance   Write down how you felt you contributed to the game. Did the coach provide you any personal feedback? Did you have any highlights? Did you have areas of improvement?

....

....

....

....

....

....

TRAINING

Date: / /

Start time :

End time :

Skills Completed
Write down the skills you worked on and developed during your training sessions.

....

....

....

....

Skills to improve
Write down areas that you can improve on for your next training session

....

....

....

....

Coach & Team Focus
Write down if your coach or team has a skill or game focus you are working on

....

....

Extra Notes
Do you have additional notes or thoughts you would like to write down?

....

....

....

GAME DAY

Date: /   /   **Start time**   :

Location: ....

Home Game ⚪   **Away Game** ⚪

Game Details

.... **Vs** ....

Game Result   Runs   Runs

Our Score   **Opposition**

Overs Bowled:

Coach Feedback

....

....

....

My Performance   Write down how you felt you contributed to the game. Did the coach provide you any personal feedback? Did you have any highlights? Did you have areas of improvement?

....

....

....

....

....

....

TRAINING

Date: / /

Start time :

End time :

Skills Completed

Write down the skills you worked on and developed during your training sessions.

....

....

....

....

Skills to improve

Write down areas that you can improve on for your next training session

....

....

....

....

Coach & Team Focus

Write down if your coach or team has a skill or game focus you are working on

....

....

Extra Notes

Do you have additional notes or thoughts you would like to write down?

....

....

....

GAME DAY

Date: / / **Start time** :

Location: ....

Home Game ○ **Away Game** ○

Game Details

.... **Vs** ....

Game Result

Our Score   Runs   **Opposition**   Runs

Overs Bowled:

Coach Feedback

....
....
....

My Performance   Write down how you felt you contributed to the game. Did the coach provide you any personal feedback? Did you have any highlights? Did you have areas of improvement?

....
....
....
....
....
....

TRAINING

Date: / /

Start time :

End time :

Skills Completed
Write down the skills you worked on and developed during your training sessions.

....

....

....

....

Skills to improve
Write down areas that you can improve on for your next training session

....

....

....

....

Coach & Team Focus
Write down if your coach or team has a skill or game focus you are working on

....

....

Extra Notes
Do you have additional notes or thoughts you would like to write down?

....

....

....

GAME DAY

Date: / /   **Start time** :

Location: ....

Home Game   **Away Game**

Game Details

.... **Vs** ....

Game Result   Runs   Runs

Our Score   **Opposition**

Overs Bowled:

Coach Feedback

....

....

....

My Performance   Write down how you felt you contributed to the game. Did the coach provide you any personal feedback? Did you have any highlights? Did you have areas of improvement?

....

....

....

....

....

....

TRAINING

Date: / /   **Start time** :

End time :

Skills Completed
Write down the skills you worked on and developed during your training sessions.

....

....

....

....

Skills to improve
Write down areas that you can improve on for your next training session

....

....

....

....

Coach & Team Focus
Write down if your coach or team has a skill or game focus you are working on

....

....

Extra Notes
Do you have additional notes or thoughts you would like to write down?

....

....

....

GAME DAY

Date: /   /   **Start time**   :

Location: ....

Home Game   ⬤   **Away Game**   ⬤

Game Details

.... **Vs** ....

Game Result   Runs   Runs

Our Score   **Opposition**

Overs Bowled:

Coach Feedback

....

....

....

My Performance

Write down how you felt you contributed to the game. Did the coach provide you any personal feedback? Did you have any highlights? Did you have areas of improvement?

....

....

....

....

....

....

TRAINING

Date: / /   **Start time** :

End time :

Skills Completed

Write down the skills you worked on and developed during your training sessions.

....

....

....

....

Skills to improve

Write down areas that you can improve on for your next training session

....

....

....

....

Coach & Team Focus

Write down if your coach or team has a skill or game focus you are working on

....

....

Extra Notes

Do you have additional notes or thoughts you would like to write down?

....

....

....

GAME DAY

Date: / / **Start time** :

Location: ....

Home Game **Away Game**

Game Details

.... **Vs** ....

Game Result Runs Runs

Our Score **Opposition**

Overs Bowled:

Coach Feedback

....

....

....

My Performance Write down how you felt you contributed to the game. Did
the coach provide you any personal feedback? Did you
have any highlights? Did you have areas of improvement?

....

....

....

....

....

....

TRAINING

Date: / /

Start time :

End time :

Skills Completed
Write down the skills you worked on and developed during your training sessions.

....

....

....

....

Skills to improve
Write down areas that you can improve on for your next training session

....

....

....

....

Coach & Team Focus
Write down if your coach or team has a skill or game focus you are working on

....

....

Extra Notes
Do you have additional notes or thoughts you would like to write down?

....

....

....

GAME DAY

Date: / / **Start time** :

Location: ....

Home Game ⚪ **Away Game** ⚪

Game Details

.... **Vs** ....

Game Result

Runs Runs

Our Score **Opposition**

Overs Bowled:

Coach Feedback

....
....
....

My Performance Write down how you felt you contributed to the game. Did the coach provide you any personal feedback? Did you have any highlights? Did you have areas of improvement?

....
....
....
....
....
....

TRAINING

Date: / /

Start time :

End time :

Skills Completed

Write down the skills you worked on and developed during your training sessions.

....

....

....

....

Skills to improve

Write down areas that you can improve on for your next training session

....

....

....

....

Coach & Team Focus

Write down if your coach or team has a skill or game focus you are working on

....

....

Extra Notes

Do you have additional notes or thoughts you would like to write down?

....

....

....

GAME DAY

Date: / /   **Start time** :

Location: ....

Home Game ⬤   **Away Game** ⬤

Game Details

.... **Vs** ....

Game Result   Runs   Runs

Our Score   **Opposition**

Overs Bowled:

Coach Feedback

....
....
....

My Performance   Write down how you felt you contributed to the game. Did the coach provide you any personal feedback? Did you have any highlights? Did you have areas of improvement?

....
....
....
....
....
....

TRAINING

Date: / /

Start time :

End time :

Skills Completed

Write down the skills you worked on and developed during your training sessions.

....

....

....

....

Skills to improve

Write down areas that you can improve on for your next training session

....

....

....

....

Coach & Team Focus

Write down if your coach or team has a skill or game focus you are working on

....

....

Extra Notes

Do you have additional notes or thoughts you would like to write down?

....

....

....

GAME DAY

Date: / /   **Start time** :

Location: ....

Home Game ⬤   **Away Game** ⬤

Game Details

.... **Vs** ....

Game Result

Our Score   Runs   **Opposition**   Runs

Overs Bowled:

Coach Feedback

....
....
....

My Performance   Write down how you felt you contributed to the game. Did the coach provide you any personal feedback? Did you have any highlights? Did you have areas of improvement?

....
....
....
....
....
....

TRAINING

Date: / /

Start time :

End time :

Skills Completed
Write down the skills you worked on and developed during your training sessions.

....

....

....

....

Skills to improve
Write down areas that you can improve on for your next training session

....

....

....

....

Coach & Team Focus
Write down if your coach or team has a skill or game focus you are working on

....

....

Extra Notes
Do you have additional notes or thoughts you would like to write down?

....

....

....

GAME DAY

Date: / /   **Start time** :

Location: ....

Home Game   **Away Game**

Game Details

.... **Vs** ....

Game Result   Runs   Runs

Our Score   **Opposition**

Overs Bowled:

Coach Feedback

....
....
....

My Performance   Write down how you felt you contributed to the game. Did the coach provide you any personal feedback? Did you have any highlights? Did you have areas of improvement?

....
....
....
....
....
....

TRAINING

Date: / /   **Start time**   :

End time   :

Skills Completed

Write down the skills you worked on and developed during your training sessions.

....

....

....

....

Skills to improve

Write down areas that you can improve on for your next training session

....

....

....

....

Coach & Team Focus

Write down if your coach or team has a skill or game focus you are working on

....

....

Extra Notes

Do you have additional notes or thoughts you would like to write down?

....

....

....

GAME DAY

Date: /   /   **Start time**   :

Location: ....

Home Game ⚪   **Away Game** ⚪

Game Details

.... **Vs** ....

Game Result   Runs   Runs

Our Score   **Opposition**

Overs Bowled:

Coach Feedback

....

....

....

My Performance   Write down how you felt you contributed to the game. Did the coach provide you any personal feedback? Did you have any highlights? Did you have areas of improvement?

....

....

....

....

....

....

TRAINING

Date: / /   **Start time**   :

End time   :

Skills Completed
Write down the skills you worked on and developed during your training sessions.

....

....

....

....

Skills to improve
Write down areas that you can improve on for your next training session

....

....

....

....

Coach & Team Focus
Write down if your coach or team has a skill or game focus you are working on

....

....

Extra Notes
Do you have additional notes or thoughts you would like to write down?

....

....

....

GAME DAY

Date: / / **Start time** :

Location: ....

Home Game   **Away Game**

Game Details

.... **Vs** ....

Game Result   Runs   Runs

Our Score   **Opposition**

Overs Bowled:

Coach Feedback

....

....

....

My Performance   Write down how you felt you contributed to the game. Did the coach provide you any personal feedback? Did you have any highlights? Did you have areas of improvement?

....

....

....

....

....

....

TRAINING

Date: / /

Start time :

End time :

Skills Completed

Write down the skills you worked on and developed during your training sessions.

....

....

....

....

Skills to improve

Write down areas that you can improve on for your next training session

....

....

....

....

Coach & Team Focus

Write down if your coach or team has a skill or game focus you are working on

....

....

Extra Notes

Do you have additional notes or thoughts you would like to write down?

....

....

....

GAME DAY

Date: /   /   **Start time**   :

Location: ....

Home Game   **Away Game**

Game Details

.... **Vs** ....

Game Result   Runs   Runs

Our Score   **Opposition**

Overs Bowled:

Coach Feedback

....

....

....

My Performance   Write down how you felt you contributed to the game. Did the coach provide you any personal feedback? Did you have any highlights? Did you have areas of improvement?

....

....

....

....

....

....

TRAINING

Date: /   /

Start time   :

End time   :

Skills Completed
Write down the skills you worked on and developed during your training sessions.

....

....

....

....

Skills to improve
Write down areas that you can improve on for your next training session

....

....

....

....

Coach & Team Focus
Write down if your coach or team has a skill or game focus you are working on

....

....

Extra Notes
Do you have additional notes or thoughts you would like to write down?

....

....

....

GAME DAY

Date: /   /   **Start time**   :

Location: ....

Home Game ⚪   **Away Game** ⚪

Game Details

.... **Vs** ....

Game Result   Runs   Runs

Our Score   **Opposition**

Overs Bowled:

Coach Feedback

....

....

....

My Performance

Write down how you felt you contributed to the game. Did the coach provide you any personal feedback? Did you have any highlights? Did you have areas of improvement?

....

....

....

....

....

....

TRAINING

Date: / /   **Start time**   :

End time   :

Skills Completed
Write down the skills you worked on and developed during your training sessions.

....

....

....

....

Skills to improve
Write down areas that you can improve on for your next training session

....

....

....

....

Coach & Team Focus
Write down if your coach or team has a skill or game focus you are working on

....

....

Extra Notes
Do you have additional notes or thoughts you would like to write down?

....

....

....

GAME DAY

Date: /   /   **Start time**   :

Location: ....

Home Game   **Away Game**

Game Details

.... **Vs** ....

Game Result   Runs   Runs

Our Score   **Opposition**

Overs Bowled:

Coach Feedback

....

....

....

My Performance   Write down how you felt you contributed to the game. Did the coach provide you any personal feedback? Did you have any highlights? Did you have areas of improvement?

....

....

....

....

....

....

TRAINING

Date: / /

Start time :

End time :

Skills Completed

Write down the skills you worked on and developed during your training sessions.

....

....

....

....

Skills to improve

Write down areas that you can improve on for your next training session

....

....

....

....

Coach & Team Focus

Write down if your coach or team has a skill or game focus you are working on

....

....

Extra Notes

Do you have additional notes or thoughts you would like to write down?

....

....

....

GAME DAY

Date: /   /   **Start time**   :

Location: ....

Home Game ○   **Away Game** ○

Game Details

.... **Vs** ....

Game Result   Runs   Runs

Our Score   **Opposition**

Overs Bowled:

Coach Feedback

....

....

....

My Performance   Write down how you felt you contributed to the game. Did the coach provide you any personal feedback? Did you have any highlights? Did you have areas of improvement?

....

....

....

....

....

....

TRAINING

Date: / /

Start time :

End time :

Skills Completed

Write down the skills you worked on and developed during your training sessions.

....

....

....

....

Skills to improve

Write down areas that you can improve on for your next training session

....

....

....

....

Coach & Team Focus

Write down if your coach or team has a skill or game focus you are working on

....

....

Extra Notes

Do you have additional notes or thoughts you would like to write down?

....

....

....

GAME DAY

Date: /   /   **Start time**   :

Location: ....

Home Game   **Away Game**

Game Details

.... **Vs** ....

Game Result   Runs   Runs

Our Score   **Opposition**

Overs Bowled:

Coach Feedback

....

....

....

My Performance   Write down how you felt you contributed to the game. Did the coach provide you any personal feedback? Did you have any highlights? Did you have areas of improvement?

....

....

....

....

....

....

TRAINING

Date: / /

Start time :

End time :

Skills Completed
Write down the skills you worked on and developed during your training sessions.

....

....

....

....

Skills to improve
Write down areas that you can improve on for your next training session

....

....

....

....

Coach & Team Focus
Write down if your coach or team has a skill or game focus you are working on

....

....

Extra Notes
Do you have additional notes or thoughts you would like to write down?

....

....

....

GAME DAY

Date: / /   **Start time** :

Location: ....

Home Game ⬤   **Away Game** ⬤

Game Details

.... **Vs** ....

Game Result   Runs   Runs

Our Score   **Opposition**

Overs Bowled:

Coach Feedback

....

....

....

My Performance   Write down how you felt you contributed to the game. Did the coach provide you any personal feedback? Did you have any highlights? Did you have areas of improvement?

....

....

....

....

....

....

TRAINING

Date: / /   **Start time**   :

                     End time   :

Skills Completed

Write down the skills you worked on and developed during your training sessions.

....

....

....

....

Skills to improve

Write down areas that you can improve on for your next training session

....

....

....

....

Coach & Team Focus

Write down if your coach or team has a skill or game focus you are working on

....

....

Extra Notes

Do you have additional notes or thoughts you would like to write down?

....

....

....

GAME DAY

Date: / /   **Start time**   :

Location: ....

Home Game ⬤   **Away Game** ⬤

Game Details

.... **Vs** ....

Game Result   Runs   Runs

Our Score   **Opposition**

Overs Bowled:

Coach Feedback

....

....

....

My Performance   Write down how you felt you contributed to the game. Did
the coach provide you any personal feedback? Did you
have any highlights? Did you have areas of improvement?

....

....

....

....

....

....

TRAINING

Date: / /   **Start time**   :

End time   :

Skills Completed

Write down the skills you worked on and developed during your training sessions.

....

....

....

....

Skills to improve

Write down areas that you can improve on for your next training session

....

....

....

Coach & Team Focus

Write down if your coach or team has a skill or game focus you are working on

....

....

Extra Notes

Do you have additional notes or thoughts you would like to write down?

....

....

....

GAME DAY

Date: / /   **Start time** :

Location: ....

Home Game ⬤   **Away Game** ⬤

Game Details

.... **Vs** ....

Game Result   Runs   Runs

Our Score   **Opposition**

Overs Bowled:

Coach Feedback

....

....

....

My Performance

Write down how you felt you contributed to the game. Did the coach provide you any personal feedback? Did you have any highlights? Did you have areas of improvement?

....

....

....

....

....

....

TRAINING

Date: / / **Start time** :

End time :

Skills Completed
Write down the skills you worked on and developed during your training sessions.

....

....

....

....

Skills to improve
Write down areas that you can improve on for your next training session

....

....

....

....

Coach & Team Focus
Write down if your coach or team has a skill or game focus you are working on

....

....

Extra Notes
Do you have additional notes or thoughts you would like to write down?

....

....

....

GAME DAY

Date: / /   **Start time** :

Location: ....

Home Game   **Away Game**

Game Details

.... **Vs** ....

Game Result

Runs   Runs

Our Score   **Opposition**

Overs Bowled:

Coach Feedback

....
....
....

My Performance   Write down how you felt you contributed to the game. Did the coach provide you any personal feedback? Did you have any highlights? Did you have areas of improvement?

....
....
....
....
....

TRAINING

Date: / /

Start time :

End time :

Skills Completed

Write down the skills you worked on and developed during your training sessions.

....

....

....

....

Skills to improve

Write down areas that you can improve on for your next training session

....

....

....

....

Coach & Team Focus

Write down if your coach or team has a skill or game focus you are working on

....

....

Extra Notes

Do you have additional notes or thoughts you would like to write down?

....

....

....

GAME DAY

Date: /   /   **Start time**   :

Location: ....

Home Game ◯   **Away Game** ◯

Game Details

.... **Vs** ....

Game Result   Runs   Runs

Our Score   **Opposition**

Overs Bowled:

Coach Feedback

....
....
....

My Performance   Write down how you felt you contributed to the game. Did the coach provide you any personal feedback? Did you have any highlights? Did you have areas of improvement?

....
....
....
....
....

TRAINING

Date: / /

Start time :

End time :

Skills Completed

Write down the skills you worked on and developed during your training sessions.

....

....

....

....

Skills to improve

Write down areas that you can improve on for your next training session

....

....

....

....

Coach & Team Focus

Write down if your coach or team has a skill or game focus you are working on

....

....

Extra Notes

Do you have additional notes or thoughts you would like to write down?

....

....

....

GAME DAY

Date: / /   **Start time** :

Location: ....

Home Game ⚪   **Away Game** ⚪

Game Details

.... **Vs** ....

Game Result

Runs   Runs

Our Score   _____   **Opposition**   _____

Overs Bowled:

Coach Feedback

....

....

....

My Performance   Write down how you felt you contributed to the game. Did the coach provide you any personal feedback? Did you have any highlights? Did you have areas of improvement?

....

....

....

....

....

....

TRAINING

Date: / /   **Start time** :

End time :

Skills Completed

Write down the skills you worked on and developed during your training sessions.

....

....

....

....

Skills to improve

Write down areas that you can improve on for your next training session

....

....

....

....

Coach & Team Focus

Write down if your coach or team has a skill or game focus you are working on

....

....

Extra Notes

Do you have additional notes or thoughts you would like to write down?

....

....

....

GAME DAY

Date: / /   **Start time** :

Location: ....

Home Game ○   **Away Game** ○

Game Details

.... **Vs** ....

Game Result   Runs   Runs

Our Score   **Opposition**

Overs Bowled:

Coach Feedback

....
....
....

My Performance   Write down how you felt you contributed to the game. Did the coach provide you any personal feedback? Did you have any highlights? Did you have areas of improvement?

....
....
....
....
....

My Cricket Journal

-Cricket-

03

SEASON NOTES

NOTES

NOTES

NOTES

NOTES

My Cricket Journal

-Cricket-

04

Autographs & Photos

Autographs & Photo's

Autographs & Photo's

Autographs & Photo's

Autographs & Photo's

Autographs & Photo's

CRICKET
Journal

The Life
Graduate
PUBLISHING GROUP

-Cricket-

CPSIA information can be obtained
at www.ICGtesting.com
Printed in the USA
BVHW091443240620
582238BV00012B/411